FRANCIS FRITH'S

TOWN & CITY

MEMORIES

BURY

TERRY ASHWORTH was born in Bury and has taken a lifetime interest in its history. He is a founder member of the Bury and District Local History Society and co-author, with the late Vernon Sandiford, of 'The Forgotten Valley', a study of the early mills of the Industrial Revolution, published in 1981. He has written and broadcast on various aspects of local history and now edits the Society's twice yearly Journal.

MARKET PLACE 1895 36782

FRANCIS FRITH'S

TOWN & CITY

MEMORIES

BURY

TERRY ASHWORTH

FRANCIS FRITH'S
TOWN & CITY
MEMORIES

First published as Bury, A Photographic History of your Town
in 2002 by Black Horse Books, an imprint of The Francis Frith Collection
Revised edition published in the United Kingdom in 2006 by
The Francis Frith Collection as Bury, Town and City Memories
Limited Hardback Edition ISBN 1-84589-154-6
Paperback Edition ISBN 1-84589-155-4

British Library Cataloguing in Publication Data

Bury
Town and City Memories
Terry Ashworth

The Francis Frith Collection®
Frith's Barn, Teffont,
Salisbury, Wiltshire SP3 5QP
Tel: +44 (0) 1722 716 376
Email: info@francisfrith.co.uk
www.francisfrith.com

Aerial photographs reproduced under licence from Simmons Aerofilms Limited
Historical Ordnance Survey maps reproduced under licence from Homecheck.co.uk

Printed and bound in England

Front Cover: **BURY, THE MARKET 1902** 48562t
The colour-tinting in this image is for illustrative purposes only,
and is not intended to be historically accurate

FRANCIS FRITH'S
TOWN & CITY
MEMORIES

CONTENTS

Francis Frith, Victorian founder of the world-famous photographic archive, was a devout Quaker and a highly successful Victorian businessman. By 1860 he was already a multi-millionaire, having established and sold a wholesale grocery business in Liverpool. He had also made a series of pioneering photographic journeys to the Nile region. The images he returned with were the talk of London. An eminent modern historian has likened their impact on the population of the time to that on our own generation of the first photographs taken on the surface of the moon.

Frith had a passion for landscape, and was as equally inspired by the countryside of Britain as he was by the desert regions of the Nile. He resolved to set out on a new career and to use his skills with a camera. He established a business in Reigate as a specialist publisher of topographical photographs.

Frith lived in an era of immense and sometimes violent change. For the poor in the early part of Victoria's reign work was a drudge and the hours long, and ordinary people had precious little free time. Most had not travelled far beyond the boundaries of their own town or village. Mass tourism was in its infancy during the 1860s, but during the next decade the railway network and the establishment of Bank Holidays and half-Saturdays gradually made it possible for the working man and his family to enjoy holidays and to see a little more of the world. With characteristic business acumen, Francis Frith foresaw that these new tourists would enjoy having souvenirs to commemorate their days out. He began selling photo-souvenirs of seaside resorts and beauty spots, which the Victorian public pasted into treasured family albums.

Frith's aim was to photograph every town and village in Britain. For the next thirty years he travelled the country by train and by pony and trap, producing fine photographs of seaside resorts and beauty spots that were keenly bought by millions of Victorians.

THE RISE OF FRITH & CO

Each photograph was taken with tourism in mind, the small team of Frith photographers concentrating on busy shopping streets, beaches, seafronts, picturesque lanes and villages. They also photographed buildings: the Victorian and Edwardian eras were times of huge building activity, and town halls, libraries, post offices, schools and technical colleges were springing up all over the country. They were invariably celebrated by a proud Victorian public, and photo souvenirs – visual records – published by F Frith & Co were sold in their hundreds of thousands. In addition, many new commercial buildings such as hotels, inns and pubs were photographed, often because their owners specifically commissioned Frith postcards or prints of them for re-sale or for publicity purposes.

In order to gain some understanding of the scale of Frith's business one only has to look at the catalogue issued by Frith & Co in 1886: it runs to some 670 pages. By 1890 Frith had created the greatest specialist photographic publishing company in the world, with over 2,000 stockists! The picture on the right shows the Frith & Co display board on the wall of the stockist at Ingleton in the Yorkshire Dales (left of window). Beautifully constructed with a mahogany frame and gilt inserts, it displayed a dozen scenes.

THE MAKING OF AN ARCHIVE

POSTCARD BONANZA

The ever-popular holiday postcard we know today took many years to appear, and F Frith & Co was in the vanguard of its development. Postcards became a hugely popular means of communication and sold in their millions. Frith's company took full advantage of this boom and soon became the major publisher of photographic view postcards.

Francis Frith died in 1898 at his villa in Cannes, his great project still growing. His sons Eustace and Cyril continued their father's monumental task, expanding the number of views offered to the public and recording more and more places in Britain, as the coasts and countryside were opened up to mass travel. The archive Frith created

continued in business for another seventy years. By 1970 it contained over a third of a million pictures of 7,000 cities, towns and villages. The massive photographic record Frith has left to us stands as a living monument to a special and very remarkable man.

This book shows Bury as it was photographed by this world-famous archive at various periods in its development over the past 150 years. Every photograph was taken for a specific commercial purpose, which explains why the selection may not show every aspect of the town landscape. However, the photographs, compiled from one of the world's most celebrated archives, provide an important and absorbing record of your town.

BURY FROM THE AIR 1933 AF42022

FROM SAXON TIMES

THE NAME BURY is derived from the Saxon, meaning 'a fortified place', and a glance at its geographical position would well support this description. The early settlers took advantage of this high bluff of land with commanding views across a broad, glacial plain. From here they could gaze out toward the Forest of Rossendale and follow the course of the River Irwell, carved out by the meltwater of the Second Ice Age.

There is evidence of habitation in the area from the late Neolithic period some 4,500 years ago. Whitelow Cairn to the east is described as an Early Bronze Age ritual site, while recent excavations at Castlesteads, to the north, have revealed evidence of an Iron Age hill fort.

During the Roman period a major military road known as Watling Street, linking Mamucium (Manchester) with the fort at Ribchester, passed a few miles to the west of Bury, through present day Radcliffe and Affetside, but there is no evidence of a settlement. A cross situated in the village of Affetside is said to be equidistant from London and Edinburgh, but has no Roman relevance and probably dates from the Middle Ages.

Following the end of the Roman Occupation, it was the Anglo-Saxon settlers who were to give an identity to the region. It is at this time that the name 'Byri' appears, meaning 'a stronghold or fortified place', and to the west, Tottington, 'the land of Tota' (probably a local chieftain). To the south the Saxon name Prestwich means roughly 'priest's retreat', and suggests a religious establishment.

Bury is not mentioned in the Domesday Book of 1086, but it is probable that a settlement and church did exist there long before the Norman Invasion. Domesday did, however, clarify the distribution of lands. Shortly after the Conquest, the Norman knight Roger de Montbegon was granted the lands between the rivers Ribble and Mersey, including the extensive manor of Tottington, of which Bury Manor was a part. Despite the town's omission from the Domesday survey, the resident de Bury family were destined for high places. Edward married Alice de Montbegon, grand-daughter of Roger, and the manor of Bury was subsequently held by their son Adam for 'one knights fee'.

Early in the 14th century Adam's descendent Alice de Bury married Roger de Pilkington, bringing together the two manors. The manor house stood on that high bluff of land once occupied by Bronze Age settlers. In 1469 royal consent was given to Thomas Pilkington to 'construct

'Byri on Irwell, 4 or v miles from Manchestre, but a poore market.
Ther is a Ruine of a Castel by the paroch chirch
yn the Towne. It longgid with the Towne
sumtime to the Pilkentons, now the Erles
of Darby. Pilkenton had a place hard
by Pilkenton parke, 3 miles from Manchestre … yarn is made thereabouts'.
JOHN LELAND 1540

walls and turrets … around and below his manor house in Bury in the County of Lancaster and to shut in the manor house with such manner of walls and turrets, also to embattle, crenellate and machiolate those towers'. Bury now had a castle.

But the Pilkingtons were Yorkists, and following the defeat of Richard III at the Battle of Bosworth in 1485 their lands were confiscated and their manor at Bury given to Thomas Stanley, the newly created Earl of Derby. But Stanley had no use for Bury Castle, and by the middle of the next century it was no more than a ruin. For many years the site was plundered for masonry as the town grew around the Market Place.

The broad moorlands beyond provided rich grazing land, and wool was to be Bury's prime industry. The population around 1660 was about 1,000, mostly dwelling around the church and the market place, but the town was hardly an inspiration to visitors. 'A market town of no great account', wrote one, while Daniel Defoe on his travels around the kingdom described it as 'a little town lying at the foot of desolate mountains'(!) But that was to change.

By the mid 1700s, technical developments in textile machinery were revolutionising the industry, and Bury was to play a major role in those achievements. Communications were opening up to cope with increasing trade; Bury's first turnpike was opened to Whalley in 1789, and the canal from Bolton and Manchester arrived in 1795. New industries were developing, notably papermaking and engineering, and by the 1830s the population had grown to around twenty thousand. The town became a Parliamentary Borough in 1832, and Improvement Commissioners were appointed in 1846.

Bury was emerging into the Victorian age.

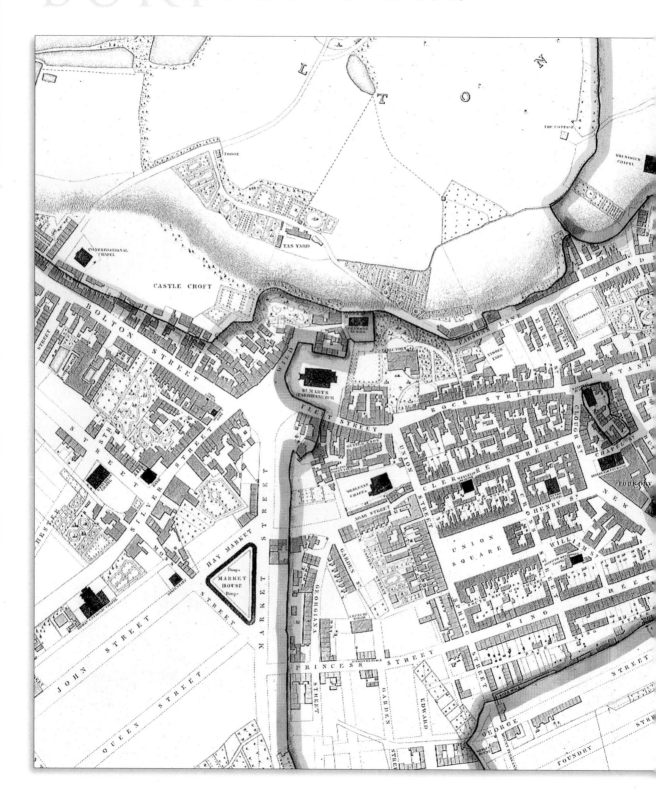

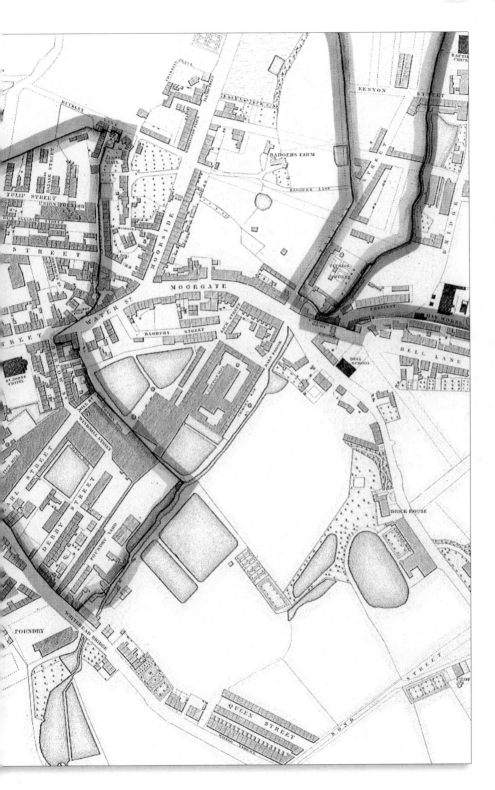

BENSON'S MAP OF
BURY 1845

*Reproduced by permission
of Bury Archive Services*

THE HISTORIC LEGACY - BURY 1902

THE MARKET PLACE AND THE CHURCH 1902 48564

The historic centre of the town at the beginning of the last century was dominated by the parish church and by the statue of Sir Robert Peel, one of the town's most famous sons. Beyond is the rambling by-way known as The Wylde, and in the foreground is the road combining two major trade routes, from Liverpool in the west to Hull in the east, and from Manchester in the south to Skipton and the Lancashire mill towns to the north. Intersecting tram tracks can be seen on the road, one leading off to the left to the depot built on the site of Bury Castle. The lamp in the foreground right was replaced in 1905 by the Lancashire Fusiliers South African War memorial. In 1916 the memorial was moved to Whitehead Gardens in Manchester Road; it was replaced by a tram shelter popularly known as 'The Umbrella'.

THE HISTORIC LEGACY - GEM OF THE DIOCESE

FROM DISCOVERIES made close by the present building, it is possible that the church of Saint Mary the Virgin stands on a Bronze Age burial site. There was certainly a Christian church there in the 13th century, and it saw the town grow over four centuries. By 1770 the nave and aisles of the medieval church had become unsafe, and it was decided to replace them with a new building in the Georgian style. This was completed in 1780, and the remaining tower and spire was replaced in 1845 by another in neo-Gothic style. This, however, produced an incongruous effect as it rose high above the squat Georgian nave, so in 1871 a committee was appointed and it was decided to rebuild the nave and to raise the steeple accordingly. A fund was set up to raise £15,000, and the architect

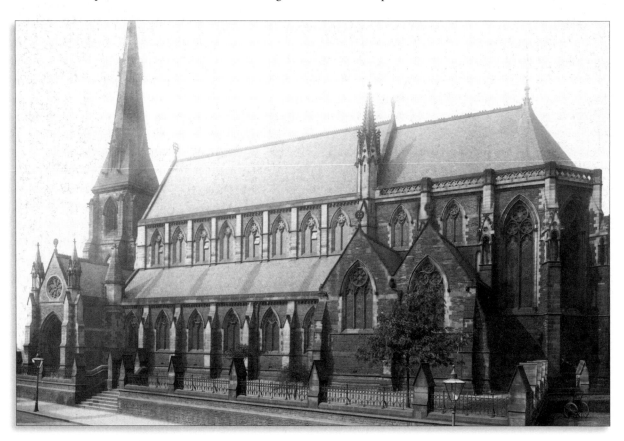

THE PARISH CHURCH 1895 36784

The Historic Legacy - Gem of the Diocese

The Church, The Choir Screen 1902 48565A

THE HISTORIC LEGACY - GEM OF THE DIOCESE

J S Crowther was retained. The result was a lavishly designed nave, which was said to have been inspired by Tintern Abbey; it was described by the Bishop of Manchester at its consecration in February 1876 as 'the gem of the Diocese'. The cost, however, was far in excess of the estimate, and nothing was left to pay for the raising of the steeple. It was expected that further funds would be forthcoming, but it was not to be, and today the nave remains visibly higher than a steeple which is some thirty years its senior.

There have been some thirty-seven rectors since the first, who was named Peter, in 1189; among them was the Rev John Stanley, younger brother of the eleventh Earl of Derby, who held the office from 1743 to 1778. He brought great wealth to the parish, and founded an Old Free Charity School for 'the teaching of such poor children residing within the town or Parish of Bury to read English and to write'. This was to become the Bury Church School, which exists to the present day. He also gained authority under the Glebe Act to lease large areas of church land for the development of a growing town. Perhaps as a result of this many of the town's streets are named after successive rectors or members of their families: Stanley, Clerke, Hornby, Edward, Geoffrey, Cecil and many more.

Under the hammer-beam roof of the south aisle hang several of the colours of the Lancashire Fusiliers, who had long historic associations with the town; several artefacts of the Regiment are to be found within the church.

THE PARISH CHURCH, INTERIOR 1895 36785

The interior of the church, which is described as 'the Gem of the Diocese'.

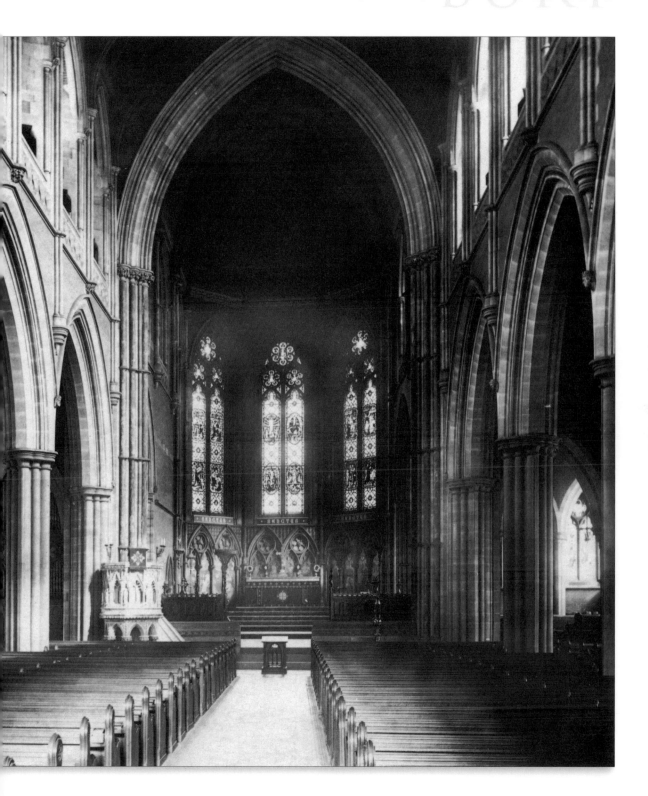

THE HISTORIC LEGACY - THE WYLDE

WHERE the statue of Sir Robert Peel stands today the Market Cross once stood, raised on three steps and bearing the arms of the ancient de Bury family. Nearby was the Court House, where the lord of the manor presided over the 'Court Leet', and unfortunate miscreants were sent for a spell in the pillory or the stocks by the church wall. For the even less fortunate there was the dungeon, whose occupants would no doubt be tormented by joyous merrymaking in the adjacent inns: the Ring o'Bells on one side, and the appropriately named Dungeon Inn on the other.

Beyond lay the meandering alley known as The Wylde, a curious name, but possibly a corruption of The Wynde, a name often given to narrow, twisting lanes. Here lay more inns and ale houses: the White Bear, the Globe, the Grey Mare, and the Crooked Billet.

Fairs were held three times a year, when there would be much sporting and feasting. But despite John Leland's sour observations, this must have been a busy place at all times. Traders would set their stalls up against the church wall, and a 19th-century painting shows stone fish slabs permanently placed around the Market Cross.

THE PARISH CHURCH C1955 B257017

This photograph of the parish church shows how the tower is lower than the roof of the nave. Because of the discrepancy, the two constructions are linked by an architectural feature known as a narthex.

THE MARKET PLACE AND THE CHURCH 1902 48564

Most of the inns and taverns in The Wylde were swept away early in the 19th century, but one of the oldest remains to the present day. The half-timbered gable end seen to the left is that of the Globe Inn, a cruck beam structure probably dating from the 17th century. Some time in the 1830s the landlord, in order to add a distinctive touch to his premises, sawed a beer barrel in two and placed the halves on the wall above the entrance. This caught the public imagination, and from thenceforward the inn has been known as the Two Tubs. Just outside the Two Tubs we can see a lamp standard carrying a distinctive white globe. This was one of Bury's bright new electric arc lamps, put up following the installation of their first power station at Whitehead Bridge in 1893. The lamps were, however, reserved for the main streets of the town, and gas lighting remained paramount for many more years. In the background we can see the house where Bury's first bank was established by Edmund and John Grundy in partnership with Abraham Wood in 1827. The bank moved to Silver Street, and for a time between 1844 and 1850 the building held the Mechanics Institute. In 1913 it became a tuberculosis clinic, and in later years broadened into a general health centre.

THE HISTORIC LEGACY - EARLY LEARNING

BEYOND The Wylde, round the back of the parish church, is the Church House, once the old Bury Grammar School (36790, below). There had been a grammar school on this site as early as 1617, and there are records of the Rev Henry Bury leaving a legacy of £300 to the school in 1634. The teaching must have been of a high quality, as several of its students later entered Cambridge University, but in later years legal disputes deprived it of most of its revenues.

In 1726 it was re-founded and re-endowed by an ex-pupil, the Rev Roger Kay, and in 1783 a new building was constructed in Georgian style. By the early years of the 19th century it had seventy-five scholars (all boys; the girls' Grammar School was not established until 1884). The annual fee was twenty shillings if a boy was taught by the Headmaster, but only ten shillings if he was taught by the undermaster, and there were two scholarships to either Oxford or Cambridge.

In 1861 a further building was added. This was styled in Victorian neo-Gothic, which gives the curious effect of seeming older than the original Georgian building. The main room was named the Blackburne Hall after a former rector, Archdeacon Foster Grey Blackburne, while another commemorates the founder Roger Kay. The Grammar School remained here until 1903, when it was transferred, together with the girls' Grammar School, to new premises in Tenterden Street. Now known as the Church House, it serves the purpose of a parish hall.

A walk round the back of these buildings provides panoramic views to the north where, with a little imagination, it is possible to appreciate the commanding position held by the original settlement.

THE GRAMMAR SCHOOL 1895 36790

The building to the left is the Georgian school of 1793, while to the centre of the picture is the neo-Gothic addition of 1861.

THE HISTORIC LEGACY - SIR ROBERT PEEL

THERE is often some confusion about Sir Robert Peel. The statue that holds a commanding position in the Market Place is that of the second baronet; it was placed there in 1852 to commemorate his repeal of the hated Corn Laws. It was his father, Sir Robert Peel the first baronet, who made a substantial contribution to the industrial development of the town. He came down from Oswaldtwistle, to the north of Bury, in 1772 to establish a partnership with Haworth and Yates, and to build some nine mills in the area concerned with cotton and calico printing. He amassed a fortune, and in 1797 donated £10,000 to the government, impoverished by the Napoleonic Wars. For this he was created a baronet and became Sir Robert Peel.

His son Robert was born at Chamber Hall in 1788, but within eleven years the family were to leave Bury and move to Tamworth in Staffordshire, where the Peels had other industrial interests. Peel, the father, became MP for Tamworth, and fought strenuously for the improvement of working conditions in factories.

He bought a seat in Parliament for his son in 1812, and Peel the younger launched into a political career, which was also to earn him a knighthood. He became Home Secretary in 1822; during his period of office he created the Metropolitan Police Force, consequently known as 'Peelers' or 'Bobbies'. Their authority was, however, limited to London - Bury, his birthplace, did not get a constabulary until 1840. In 1846, during his office as Prime Minister, he fought successfully to repeal the Corn Laws. It is in gratitude for this that a statue was placed in Bury Market Place, and a tower erected on Holcombe Hill.

The Peel Statue 1902 Detail From 48564

CHAMBER HALL, THE BIRTHPLACE OF SIR ROBERT PEEL 1895 36793

During their stay in Bury, the Peel family lived at Chamber Hall, situated a short distance from the centre of the town, though strictly in the township of Elton. The original house was Jacobean, built in 1611, and was occupied by John Greenhalgh, steward to the Earl of Derby, who also occupied Brandlesholme Hall. Chamber Hall was later rebuilt in the Georgian style; it is said that the family was living in a nearby cottage during work at the Hall when young Robert was born in 1788. In later years it became a Baptist Theological College, but it was demolished in 1907 when the new electricity power station was built on the site.

THE GROWING TOWN - MAKING TRACKS

SITUATED at the convergence of two major roads, Bury was well served by public transport. By 1817 there were daily coach services to Manchester and Liverpool, and on six days of the week to Burnley, Colne and Skipton, and even to far-distant Hull. Also there were twice-daily carrier services to the Yorkshire towns, north to Carlisle and across the Scottish border.

The East Lancashire Railway opened a line to Rawtenstall and Accrington in 1846, and set up their head office at Bury's Bolton Street station. Two years later another company opened an east-west route from Bury to Liverpool, and the town was firmly on the railway map. This brought to an end the era of long-distance coach services, but horse omnibuses were to provide local connections for many years to come. Regular services ran to Whitefield and Tottington.

In 1880, however, a scheme was put forward to construct a vast network of steam tramways linking the major towns north of Manchester. This led to intense negotiations between the various local authorities and interested private companies, and in 1881 the Manchester, Bury, Rochdale and Oldham Steam Tramways Limited was established. The first tram from

Left: DETAIL FROM THE MARKET PLACE 1895 36783

The imposing facade of Castle Buildings, situated on the west side of the Market Place, stands on the site of inns and shops which once clustered around the ancient cross. These historic buildings were swept away in the 1870s to make way for this characteristically Victorian edifice. Through the central archway there was a yard, and above it were stables approached by a ramp. No doubt there would also have been a farrier in attendance to serve the needs of busy horse traffic, and for many years there was also a vet, to whom many would bring their ailing pets.

Opposite: A STEAM TRAM 1902 48564x

A Wilkinson steam locomotive and car near the parish church on the narrow gauge Limefield to Tottington route. Track laid for both standard and narrow gauge can be seen crossing the line in the foreground. The track led to the depot in The Wylde built on the site of Bury Castle.

Bury to Broughton, north of Manchester, ran on 12 May 1883. Lines to Heywood and Rochdale followed a year later.

Not everyone was happy. The Rector objected strongly to the smoky, lumbering steam trams passing close to the parish church, particularly as the road was quite narrow at that time. The result was that trams on the Limefield service had to terminate at Clough Street, some distance away, and were drawn by horses, a situation that brought about many protests. A steam service was introduced in 1886 following the widening of the street.

The first steam trams were slow, ponderous and grossly under-powered. Timetables were often abandoned, and services ran hours late. Poor management and conflict with the local authorities were a common feature in the years that followed, and by the turn of the century the prospect of electric power beckoned. This time the local authorities were determined to take control.

Bury Corporation gained powers to construct an electric tramway in 1899, but more years of acrimonious negotiations took place before an agreement to take over the old steam lines was reached. The Corporation opened its own independent line along the Rochdale road from Moorside to Fairfield in 1903, and in the following year steam trams were withdrawn from Heap Bridge and Tottington. The new authority standardised the track gauge, and had an extension built from Limefield to Walmersley and from Fairfield to Jericho.

It was possible to travel considerable distances across south Lancashire by tram in subsequent years, but then a new challenge arose with the arrival of the motor omnibus. Bury's first bus service was opened to Walshaw in 1925, and the tram routes began to shrink. Their demise was delayed by the Second World War, but in February 1949 the last tram ran to Walmersley and an era was at an end.

THE GROWING TOWN - FLEET STREET

TO THE WEST of the Market Place, Bury Lane led down to the bridge over the River Irwell, but there were few dwellings there. As the town grew, it spread to the east along a winding road towards Moorside and beyond, over the moors toward Rochdale. The rector, Thomas Gipps, describes the road in some detail in his Terrier of 1696 as a place flanked by cottages and orchards. He refers to it simply as 'the street', and even until recent times the Market Place would be known locally as 'Top o't' Street'. The name Fleet may have resulted from its proximity to the town ditch, commonly known as a fleet. Yet the name applied to only a short stretch of the road as far as Tithebarn Street, close to the rectory. Beyond it became Rock Street, possibly a derivation of Rochdale Street, and beyond that Stanley Street, named after the Rev John Stanley, the rector of Bury in the mid 18th century, who had leased much glebe land in this part of the town. The final stretch toward Moorgate and the tollbooth was named Water Street, though the reason for this is obscure - the nearest water course was Barnbrook, some distance away.

The whole thoroughfare still retained much of its early character at the beginning of the 19th century. The clusters of cottages and their strips of land were still as Gipps described them, stretching north into the ancient Smithyfield or south into the Little Churchfield, the crowded yards and courts flanked by the humble dwellings of the poor.

FLEET STREET 1895 36780

In the distance we can see a steam tram approaching the passing loop outside Downham's premises.

But much of this, particularly in Fleet Street, was to be swept away by the radical improvements of the Victorian era, when the road was widened and straightened. Tall, new, elegant buildings were built, and leading local businesses were established, though the terms of the leases did not permit manufacture. At the age of 22, Joseph Downham took over Henry Peel's ironmongery shop in Fleet Street in 1853. The business flourished, and the fine building to be seen to the right of photograph 36780, pages 28-29, was erected in 1891. It served both the domestic market and the broader needs of industry for several decades until the business was taken over in 1969; the building was demolished two years later.

FLEET STREET 1895 36780c

To the left of the picture is the shop of W S Barlow, described in an 1889 Directory as 'Steam Printer, Stationer and Account Book Manufacturer'. The shop and works were situated in a five-storey building on the site of the Old Red Lion Hotel, demolished during the road widening in 1877. Tommy Thompson, the local author and broadcaster, was once employed there as a bookbinder. Next door were the premises of Giles Hewart, silk mercer and linen draper. Beyond the deceptively small shop front the building contained 14 rooms, and the business employed 40 assistants. Hewart's son, Gordon, was to become one of Bury's famous sons. Born in 1870, he was called to the Bar in 1902. He took silk as a K C in 1912 and was knighted when he was appointed Solicitor General in 1916. He entered Parliament in 1918 and became a Cabinet Minister in 1921. He reached the peak of his legal career a year later when he became Lord Chief Justice of England and was created 1st Baron Hewart of Bury.

THE GROWING TOWN - THE ROCK

THE ROCK is another curious name, like the Wylde. But when did The Rock become The Rock? Officially in 1935, when the Borough Council decreed that the whole length of the road from the parish church to Moorgate, hitherto Fleet Street, Rock Street, Stanley Street and Water Street, would become The Rock. But the deeds for a house at No 151 placed it in The Rock as early as 1910. The local Chamber of Trade appealed for a common name for the four streets in 1923, showing a preference for Fleet Street. Other suggestions included High Street, or 'something with an Avenue in it'. It would seem, however, that The Rock had already drifted into common usage, and the local authority was only acknowledging the inevitable.

The widening of Fleet Street in the 1880s had progressed no further than Tithebarn Street, probably because the congestion of narrow streets to the south made clearance a difficult and expensive problem. But the will was still there, and when a new row of shops to be called Hornby Buildings (after another of Bury's rectors) was built in 1935, it was set back to the revised building line. Parts of The Rock remain narrow today, but most of it is now pedestrianised.

THE ROCK C1955 B257003

The buildings on the north side of The Rock presented a variety of styles. Dominant amongst them is the distinctive building of Burtons, 'The Tailor of Taste'. Next door, the sunblind protects the produce at the Maypole dairy, and beyond that is a very modest branch of Boots the Chemist. Later Boots had a larger two-storey building built on the site; but in the 1970s, together with Burtons, they moved out of The Rock to the new Millgate Shopping Centre.

The Rock c1955 B257022

This view shows the narrowing of the road beyond Tithebarn Street. National retailers, among them Stead and Simpson and Woolworth's, had now established themselves, but Joseph Downham's ironmongers was still flourishing at the corner of Union Street. The gap in the rows of buildings in the distance is where Hornby Buildings had been set back to the revised building line. The building beyond the gap, at the corner of Clough Street, occupies the site of Bury's first National School.

THE GROWING TOWN - IN THE FIFTIES

DETAIL FROM MARKET PLACE C1955 B257017

Memories of the First World War were deeply held in Bury, home of the Lancashire Fusiliers, who earned the distinction of 'six VCs before breakfast' in the landing at Gallipoli. On Armistice Day in 1924 a war memorial, erected by the parish church, was unveiled by Mrs Peachment, whose son, George Stanley Peachment, had been posthumously awarded the Victoria Cross during the war. Regular soldiers and Territorials, many of whom had fought side by side in the trenches, attended the ceremony, together with civic leaders.

MARKET PLACE C1955 B257019

The Market Place in the fifties would still have been recognisable to a visitor from the Edwardian era. The parish church remained unaltered, the Two Tubs still stood at the corner of Castle Street and 'Bobby' Peel still stood on his plinth (though now above a gentleman's toilet). But the trams had long gone, and the buses had departed elsewhere, though curiously the Bury Corporation Transport offices still remained in Castle Buildings (to the left of the picture). The ancient highway through the town, now the combined A56 and A58, was still busy with modern traffic, as Bury had yet to benefit from its by-passes, but the trees had grown in the churchyard and seats and shrubs had been placed on the broadened pavement outside the Derby Hotel. The Market Place had once more become a place to watch the world go by.

THE GROWING TOWN - THE TOWN HALL THAT NEVER WAS

MUCH of the land to the east of the town was glebe or church land, but to the west it was owned by the Earl of Derby. Lord Derby, eager to contribute to the rising fortunes of the town, had a new market built in 1839 on a stretch of land some way to the south of the old Market Place. But it was not popular, possibly because it was difficult to reach from the traditional centre. To solve this problem he had the Grey Mare Inn, one of the town's leading coaching inns, demolished and a new road driven through from the old Market Place to the new building.

He then flanked the road, to be known as Market Street, with a sequence of elegant buildings designed by a leading Victorian architect, Sydney Smirke. On the corner facing the Market Place was the Derby Hotel (36782, pages 40-41) which was to become the meeting place of many local organisations; it also entertained royal visitors, including King George V and Edward, the Prince of Wales, on their visits to the town. It first opened for business in February 1850, and survived until 1965. It was then demolished, and Ribblesdale House, incorporating shops and a medical centre, was built on the site.

Next to that was the Town Hall (36781, opposite) - except that it never was a town hall. The town's Commissioners, jealously guarding their independence, declined the use of the Earl's property, and the building became a court house and police station. In 1925 it was sold to the

Corporation, who subsequently used it for banquets and social events. Today it is the MET Arts Centre.

The third of Smirke's buildings was the Athenæum, a centre of learning renowned for its lectures, concerts and theatrical productions for over a century. It was taken over by the local authority in 1957, but plans to restore the declining building came to nothing and it was demolished in 1971. The name, however, survives in the new building occupied by local government offices - Athenæum House.

MARKET STREET AND THE TOWN HALL 1895 *36781*

MARKET PLACE 1895 36782

MARKET PLACE 1895 *36782*

*Caps and bowler hats aptly reflect the Victorian social order
outside the Derby Hotel in Market Street.*

Lancashire County Map

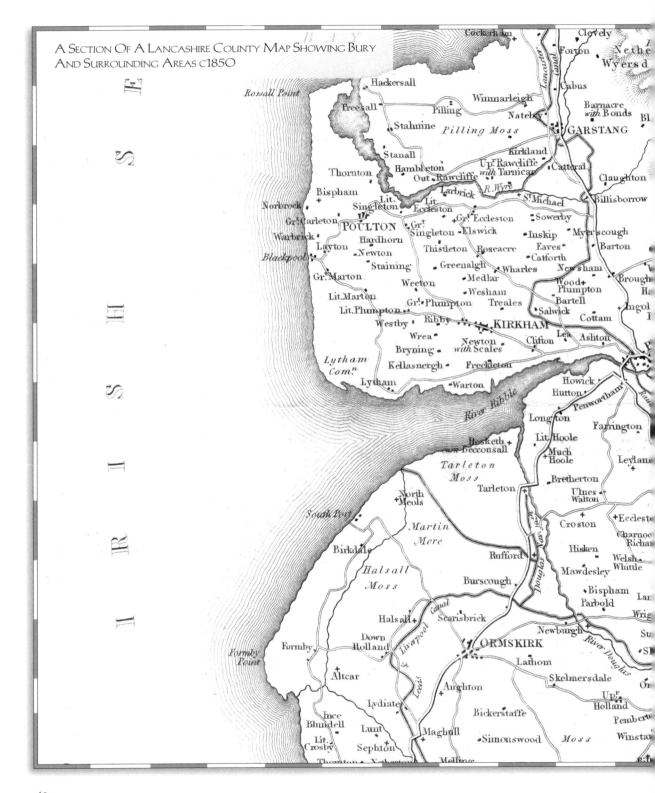

A Section Of A Lancashire County Map Showing Bury And Surrounding Areas c1850

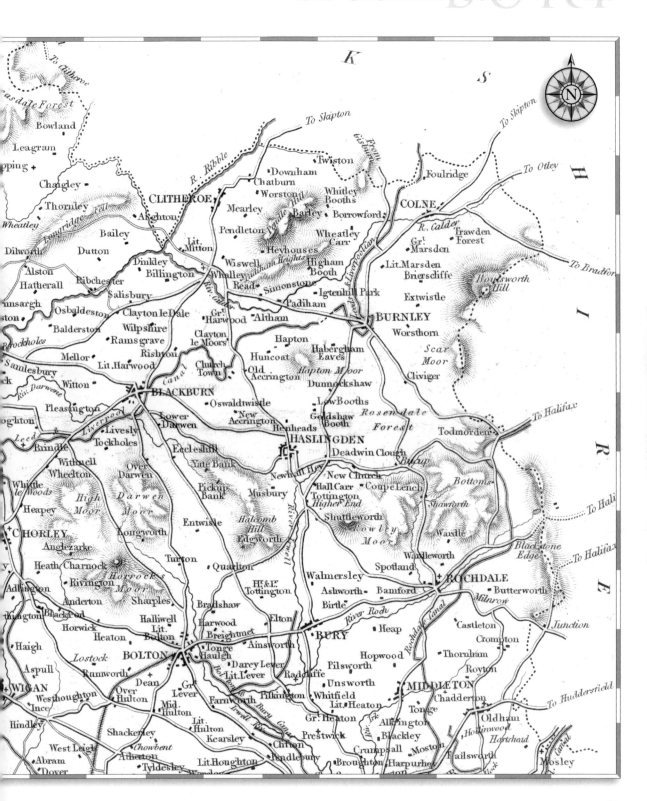

MARKETS AND GARDENS - KAY GARDENS

KAY GARDENS C1955 B257016

Kay Gardens occupies the site of the Earl of Derby's market of 1839. When the new market was opened in 1901, the old building was demolished, and the land lay derelict for some time. Various proposals were put forward suggesting a use for the site, but in 1903 it was agreed that gardens should be laid out and a memorial be erected to John Kay. Kay was a Bury-born man whose invention of the 'flying shuttle', patented in 1733, made a major contribution to the production of woven cloth. The monument was a gift to the town from a local benefactor, Henry Whitehead, who claimed to be a direct descendent of Kay. Beyond the monument is the Bury and District Co-operative Society 'Emporium'. The Co-operative movement came to Bury in 1885 with a single shop in Market Street. The movement expanded and diversified, but its various shops remained scattered. In the 1930s, work began on a new store in Market Street to bring them together. The Second World War halted work on the building, and the 'Emporium' was not opened until peace was restored in the 1940s. In later years Co-op services were again fragmented, and the store was sold to private retailers.

The tiled frontage of the Royal Cinema at the corner of Princess Street conceals the ornate facade of Bury's first custom-built theatre. The Theatre Royal was opened at Christmas in 1899 with a performance of 'Little Red Riding Hood'; later many leading actors appeared there, among them a very young Charlie Chaplin in 'The Mumming Birds'. The building was constructed by James Byrom, a local firm, and had one of the largest stages outside London, allowing dramatic presentations featuring horse races, sandstorms, earthquakes and even a train crash! It became a cinema in 1933, and flourished during the hey-day of picture-going. Patrons would take tea in the cafe overlooking Kay Gardens before seeing the show. But with the advent of television, attendances declined. The Royal Cinema was absorbed into larger groups to become first the Essoldo, then the Classic. It became twin cinemas to attract the audiences, but to no avail, and the building was demolished in the 1990s to be replaced with a bank and an amusement arcade.

MARKETS AND GARDENS - BURY'S FAMOUS MARKET

THE EARL of Derby's market of 1839 was a forbidding building surrounded by high walls. It was not popular with traders, who were accustomed to the open spaces around the old Market Place, and for a time it was occupied by a company of foot soldiers. In 1867 a glass and iron roof was added. But over the years this became neglected and unsafe, and traders were obliged to move out and set their stalls up against the walls.

In 1901 a new market hall, with a distinctive dome (48562, below) was opened across the road, together with a large open market covering much of the old fairground. It was a place of civic pride - the Borough coat of arms was carved over the main entrance - and it was to prove very popular with the public.

The Hall was open every day except Sunday and Tuesday, while the open market was open on Saturdays. It grew to be one of the largest markets in Lancashire,

THE MARKET 1902 48562

In this early photograph, tramlines can be seen turning from Market Street into Princess Street (on the left) and leading to the depot in Rochdale Road.

where all manner of things could be bought, not least the famous Bury black pudding. Within the Market Hall was a labyrinth of stalls, among them James Lawless, ironmongers, and Goslings, where treacle toffee was sold from trays.

More familiar names were to be found above the shops around the outside of the building; Berry's the florists and seedsmen, and Halsteads the grocers, where the aroma of freshly ground coffee wafted temptingly through the door.

MARKETS AND GARDENS - BURY'S FAMOUS MARKET

The Market Hall was destroyed in a disastrous fire on a Sunday morning in November 1968, and the building was gutted. The dome survived, but it was unsafe and had to be demolished. By now a new Market Hall was under construction a short distance away in the new shopping centre, and a temporary structure was built within the shell of the old building to house the traders until the new one was complete. The site was then cleared, and a new train and bus interchange was constructed.

KAY GARDENS C1955 B257006

For many years, as bus services grew, it had been the intention of the local authorities to build a bus station. Large tracts of land resulting from clearances in an area known as The Mosses had been set aside in the 1930s, but nothing was done, and the buses continued to congregate around the perimeter of Kay Gardens. On the right, on the corner of Broad Street, was the Bury Transport canteen and offices. On the opposite corner was Cox's Old English Restaurant. The restaurant was in the basement, while at street level was the shop selling delicious UCP tripe.

Set in the wall above the shop is a stone on which is carved the words 'Corn Market', while the adjacent road is still called The Haymarket. Bury Shopping Centre further along the road was an optimistically-named development on the site of a disastrous fire in the 30s. Perhaps it is best remembered for Colson's Milk Bar, a popular meeting place for teenagers in the 40s and 50s. Behind we can see the chimney of the School of Arts and Crafts, designed in the style of an Italian campanile by local architects Maxwell and Tuke (who also designed Blackpool Tower).

MARKETS AND GARDENS - WHITEHEAD GARDENS

THE WHITEHEAD CLOCK TOWER c1955 B257004

On the approach to the town from the south are the Whitehead Gardens, dominated by an imposing clock tower made of Portland stone. It was the gift of the town's ubiquitous benefactor Henry Whitehead, who had it erected in memory of his brother Walter. Walter was eminent in the field of medicine, becoming a Fellow of the Royal College of Surgeons and later President of the British Medical Association. In contrast, their brother Robert invented the torpedo. The gardens were opened in June 1914, and the opening ceremony was performed by another famous surgeon, Sir Frederick Treves. It is said that Mr Whitehead's grandson started the clock. In 1920 the Fusilier memorial of the South African War, which had stood in the Market Place since 1905, was re-erected in the gardens. In the distance we can see the Town Hall, and to the left of the memorial is the chimney of the municipal baths in St Mary's Place. There is a medical link with the site of Whitehead Gardens, as they were built over the grounds of Belle Vue, once the residence of Dr William Goodlad, who owned a private lunatic asylum.

PRIDE AND ACHIEVEMENT - MUNICIPALITY

LOCAL GOVERNMENT in Bury can perhaps be traced back to the Vestry Committees of the 18th century, but by the early 19th century the population of the town had grown to some 20,000 and the old system could not cope. In 1832 the town had become a Parliamentary Borough, and in 1846 the Bury Improvement Act was passed. Twenty-five commissioners were appointed, and they set about their task with enthusiasm, securing a £2,000 loan from Bury Banking Company and appointing a surveyor to report on the state of the town.

In 1871 it was decided to petition for Incorporation. This was at first rejected, but a charter was finally granted in 1876 and the first meeting was held on 9 February of that year - but not in the Earl of Derby's Town Hall in Market Street. Jealously guarding their independence, they met in subsequent years over a bank in Silver Street.

Departments were scattered around the town, and in the 1930s it was decided to build a Town Hall in Knowsley Street. Plans were drawn up, and a foundation stone was laid (ironically) by the Earl of Derby on 14 July 1939. Work had begun on the building a year earlier, and it continued until 1940 when the outer shell was complete. For the remainder of the war years, it remained unoccupied apart from an air raid precautions room in the basement. Work recommenced in 1947, and the Town Hall (B257020, below) was officially opened by the new Queen Elizabeth II on 22 October 1954.

THE TOWN HALL C1955 B257020

PRIDE AND ACHIEVEMENT
- A STROLL ALONG SILVER STREET

THE ROMAN CATHOLIC CHURCH 1895 36788

WALKING FROM Whitehead Gardens, past the Town Hall we come to Silver Street and the impressive lantern tower of Saint Marie's Roman Catholic Church. The church was built in 1841 at a time when the Catholic population in the town was increasing, mainly owing to Irish immigration. The lantern feature was copied from Ely Cathedral, and the architect was John Harper of York, who had family connections in Bury. Harper also designed two other Bury churches: St Paul's, Bell and All Saints', Elton. When the photograph was taken neither the Textile Hall (36791, page 56) nor the Library and Art Gallery (48561, page 57) had been built, and the land to the left was a part of Broom Hall, home of the Hutchinsons, who were local industrialists.

Maybe the name Silver Street arose because of its close association with banking. In 1836 Edmund and John Grundy, together with Abraham Wood, had established the Bury Banking Company in The Wylde, but as the business grew they moved to John Grundy's house in Silver Street. A large, ornate building was then built next door, and the bank moved there in 1867. It later became the Lancashire and Yorkshire Bank, then Martins; today it is a branch of Barclays. John Grundy's house was rebuilt, and became the Royal Hotel. The Bury Savings Bank was also established

PRIDE AND ACHIEVEMENT - A STROLL ALONG SILVER STREET

in Silver Street, occupying premises on the opposite corner of the appropriately-named Bank Street in 1850. It became the Trustee Savings Bank, and moved up the road to new premises in 1966. It is now in the 'banking quarter' of The Rock.

Silver Street was an extension of Manchester Road, and carried busy traffic from the south. The Eagle and Child was an important coaching inn with extensive stables, and there were several houses belonging to notable citizens of the town. There was also a militia barracks and parade ground.

THE UNITARIAN CHURCH AND THE SCHOOL
1895 36789

Presbyterianism came to Bury in 1719, when a meeting house was built at the corner of Bank Street and Silver Street. It was known as the Bury Chapel to distinguish it from the Bury (parish) church. The minister was the Rev Franklin Howarth, whose persuasive preaching often attracted congregations of several hundred, despite his occasional drift from Unitarianism to Methodism. A second larger chapel was built in 1837, but it was seriously undermined by the building of the East Lancashire Railway station close by. In consequence it had to be rebuilt. The new building survived until 1970, when a new chapel in radical modern style was built close by. A local authority building, Craig House, now stands on the site of the old chapel.

THE TEXTILE HALL 1895 36791

Although Bury had a greater diversity of industries than many other Lancashire towns, textiles remained prominent. So too did a proliferation of trade unions to represent the workers. In 1893 the Textile Hall was built to bring together their various offices under one roof. It was officially opened on 5 May the following year by Lady Emilia Dyke, a philanthropist and campaigner for the rights of cotton operatives. The stone carvings on the front of the building illustrate various aspects of the textile industry. Today the tower and railings have gone, and the building belongs to the Bury Metro Libraries Department. The tram tracks visible at the bottom of the picture carried the steam trams to Manchester.

PRIDE AND ACHIEVEMENT - THE WRIGLEY LEGACY

THOMAS WRIGLEY of Bridge Hall Mills, in the 1860s probably the largest paper manufacturing company in the British Empire (and by inference the world), amassed a large collection of valuable paintings, including works by Turner, Cox, Constable and Landseer. When he died in 1880 they remained with the family until 1897, the year of Queen Victoria's Jubilee, when it was decided to offer them to the town. The condition was that a suitable building should be provided, and the local authority immediately launched a competition for a design for both an art gallery and a public library (48561, below). It was won by the architects Woodhouse and Willoughby of Manchester, and the foundation stone was laid by Thomas Wrigley's eldest son Oswald Osmond on 29 April 1899. On the same occasion Oswald had conferred upon him the Freedom of the Borough, an honour of which his father would have been justly proud. The building was constructed by a local firm, Thompson and Brierley, and was opened by the Earl of Derby on 9 October 1901 amid much celebration.

Responding to government measures to provide adequate technical training for children, Bury Council established a Technical School in Broad Street in 1894 (36792, page 58). The subjects taught were closely related to the needs of local industry and commerce: cotton spinning and weaving, machine making, and paper manufacture. Local mills supplied machinery for training purposes, and a small weaving shed was reconstructed within the school. In addition there were classes in maths and English, shorthand, book keeping and foreign languages, some thirty classes in all.

THE ART GALLERY 1902
48561

The opening of the Bury art gallery and public library completed a trio of fine buildings, together with the Textile Hall and St Marie's Church, on the approach to the town. The site had previously been occupied by Broom Hall, the home of the Hutchinsons.

PRIDE AND ACHIEVEMENT - ART AND CRAFTS

IN 1896 a School of Art was established in the upper rooms of the building, and in 1900 facilities were provided for the training of pupil teachers. This continued until 1911, when the Bury Municipal Secondary School was opened and classes were transferred there, together with other commercial subjects.

The Broad Street School continued with technical training and art until the late 1940s, when the new college in Market Street, occupied by the Ministry of Defence during the war years, was released to the local authority and technical classes were transferred.

The Art School continued to occupy the upper rooms of the 'Old Tech', but ceased full-time courses in 1956. It then turned to non-vocational courses, and became known as the Bury School of Arts and Crafts. Between 1960 and 1964 its attendance grew from 750 to 3,000 under its enterprising Principal, Alan Childs, and it became one of the most successful non-vocational centres in the country. Yet despite its sustained popularity, it has frequently been threatened with closure and finally in December 2004 the local authority moved the facilities elsewhere and work began to convert the building to a museum of the Regiment of Fusiliers.

THE TECHNICAL SCHOOL 1895 36792

PRIDE AND ACHIEVEMENT - THE POST

THE ORIGINS of a postal service in Bury are not clear. There may have been facilities for receipt and despatch at Mrs Hutton's shop near the Rectory Gates in the latter years of the 18th century. However, it is known that Thomas Cooper, a victualler, operated a post office from an inn, possibly the Hare and Hounds in Millgate, near the Market Place, in 1791. When Thomas died in 1801 his wife took over the business.

From 1806 letters would be delivered free around the centre of the town, but a charge would be made for addresses beyond. This would involve the postman working long hours and travelling long distances. He would start his 'walk' around 6.00am, and would perhaps have covered over thirty miles with his bag of letters before returning by 6.00pm.

The introduction of the Penny Post in 1841 greatly increased the service, and in 1850 a new Bury Post Office was opened in Broad Street. It was to remain there for 50 years, having been rebuilt and refurbished in 1873.

Before the end of the century the search was on for new premises. The GPO favoured the site of Broom Hall,

THE POST OFFICE 1902 48563

where the art gallery and public library was subsequently built, but the eventual choice was Crompton Street, off The Rock. A new imposing building (48563, page 60) was constructed and opened on 27 August 1900. It provided a large public counter facility together with sorting and distribution services, and in 1912 a telephone exchange was installed on the first floor.

The exchange moved to new premises in 1961, but the Post Office remained until the mid-nineties, when it was incorporated into a local store.

In July of 2005 the store's lease expired and for a time the town was without a central post office.

CHESHAM GREEN 1895 36801

A tranquil rural backwater away from the industrial scene, Chesham provided a suitable retreat for some of the town's leading mill-owners. Thomas Haslam of Hudcar Mills lived at Chesham House in 1826, and in the 1840s it was occupied by Oliver Ormerod Walker, another leading industrialist, whose brother Richard was Bury's first MP. The cottages at Chesham Green were, during the same period, the residence of John Just, the deputy head at Bury Grammar School, who was also an authority on Roman Britain. The cottages were rebuilt towards the end of the 19th century.

THE INFIRMARY 1895 36797

PRIDE AND ACHIEVEMENT - THE INFIRMARY

THERE HAD been several doctors practising in Bury in the 18th century, many travelling several miles daily on horseback, but in 1829 a dispensary was established in the premises of the Hope and Anchor Inn in Bury Lane (later Bolton Street). It was supported by wealthy mill owners and public subscription, and would provide medicines and treatment for the poor but 'would admit nobody with the means to pay'.

Its services were, however, in great demand, and with no in-patient facility a new dispensary was soon needed. Land was granted at the corner of Moss Lane

and Knowsley Street, and a new building (now the Athenæum Club) was opened in 1841. But with a rapidly increasing population, the pressure grew for yet larger premises, prompting Lord Derby to give five acres of land at Littlewood Cross for the site of a new infirmary. With financial support from private donors, including a legacy of £4,000 from Thomas Norris and £10,000 from the estate of Thomas Wrigley, the building (36797, above) was completed and opened on 25 March 1882.

In 1915 Oswald Osmond, the eldest son of Thomas Wrigley, had an isolation ward built at the Infirmary in memory of his wife Annie, and in 1923 a children's ward was added as a memorial to the fallen of the First World War. Thus the Infirmary grew, still sustained by benefactors and public subscriptions until the coming of the National Health Service in 1948. By then the Infirmary, now to be known as Bury General Hospital, had grown far beyond the original group of buildings.

By the 1990s the hospital could expand no further, and it was decided to centre all departments at Bury's other hospital at Fairfield, where there was more room for expansion. Bury General finally closed its doors in September 2001.

ORDNANCE SURVEY MAP

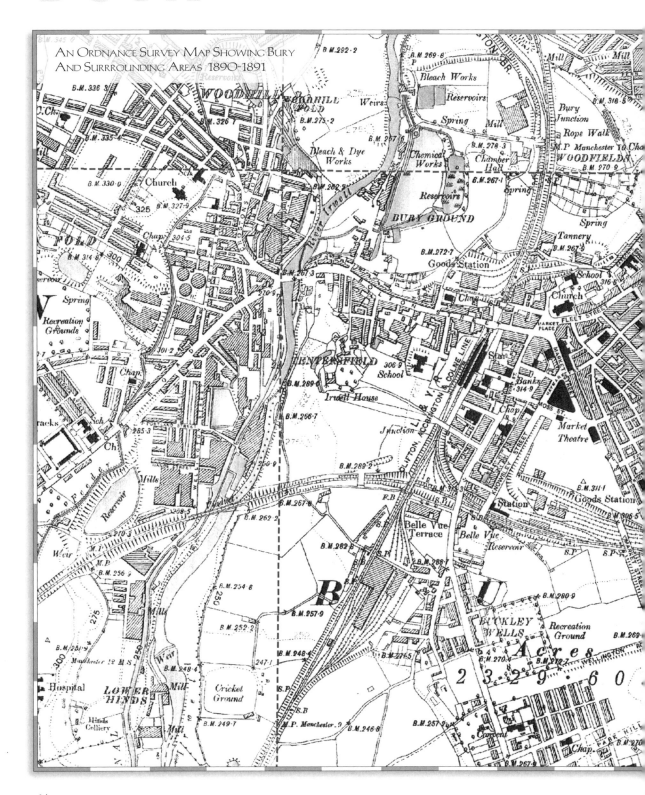

An Ordnance Survey Map Showing Bury
And Surrrounding Areas 1890-1891

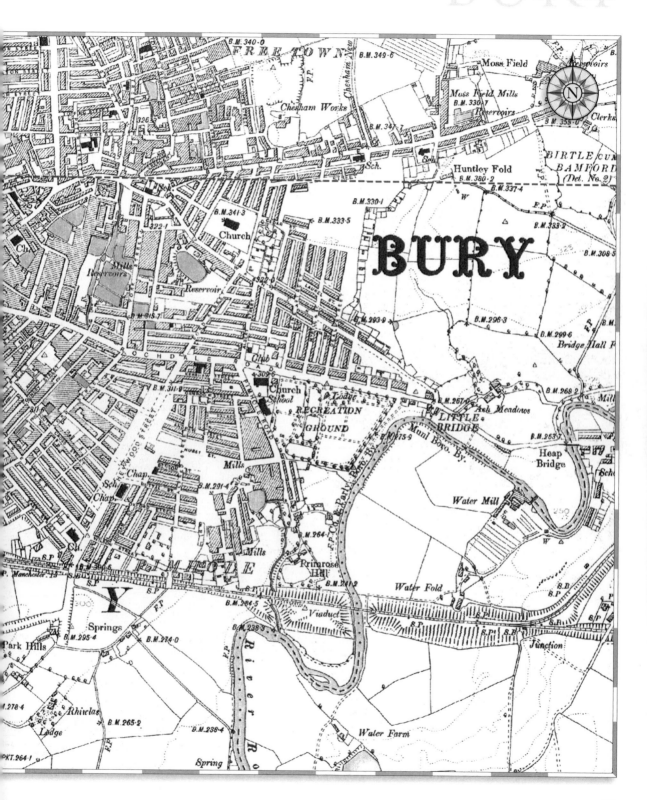

RURAL BURY - BIRTLE

THE PARISH CHURCH of St John the Baptist at Birtle stands high on the moors above Bury amid a typical rural community. But when it was built in 1846, it lay on the edge of a thriving industry operating in the valley beyond. By now the cottage worker had yielded to the factory system, and some 14 mills were threaded along the modest Cheesden Brook, most involved with cotton. This is clearly reflected in the marriage registers of Birtle church. The first entry is that of a spinner, to be followed by those of a reeler, a grinder and a weaver. There is also a collier from one of several small mines. A plaque commemorating the opening of the church bears the names of Thomas Ramsbottom and James Haworth, both owners of the valley mills.

The church at that time was simply designated as a chapelry, and its first minister, the Reverend Thomas Wilson, was variously described as an eccentric or a rogue. He nevertheless became the church's vicar, and remained in office until 1891.

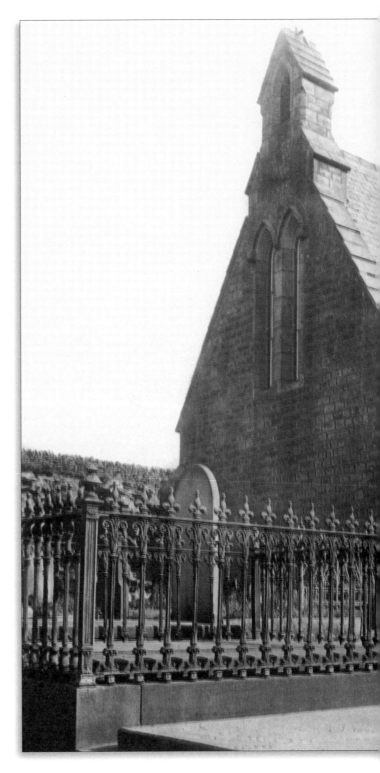

BIRTLE CHURCH 1895 36803

HERCULES FARM 1895 36802

Some of the narrow lanes that thread across the rising ground above Chesham link small settlements which probably date from Saxon times. Their names, too, hold an ancient resonance: Birchen Bower, Ninevah and Sillinghurst, the last a Saxon word for a clearing in a wood. But Hercules has little to do with Greek mythology. It derives from the Herculist, which in part may be a corruption of 'ask', the old word for an ash, which again suggests a wooded clearing. The farm stands close to the source of the Gypsy Brook, which would soon flow off the moors and down into the industrial complex of Freetown.

RURAL BURY - WALMERSLEY

SOME two miles out of Bury the old coach road to the north climbed steeply through the district of Walmersley. There had been a scattering of settlements here since ancient times. It is said that the area known as Glorybutts celebrated the success of local archers at Agincourt.

Over the centuries the principal occupation of the people was hand-loom weaving, and for many years this survived the coming of the factory system.

John Hall, who established a cotton spinning mill at Nangreaves on the old coach road in 1830, employed over 1,300 cottage weavers in the 'putting out' system. But when the development of machinery drew the workers into the factory, Hall built a 'model village' for them and named it Mount Pleasant.

In 1789 the new Bury to Whalley turnpike, built by the celebrated Blind Jack Metcalfe of Knaresborough, was completed to Walmersley and terminated at a toll

WALMERSLEY CHURCH 1895 36804
Walmersley church before the building of the tower and spire.

house at the junction with the old road. The building still stands as the local Post Office.

By the early years of the 19th century industry was growing rapidly, particularly along the valleys that flanked the district. Know Mill was built close to Bevis Green, where itinerant woollen weavers once rented basement workshops. There were cotton mills at Limefield and Lumm, and a bleachworks at Longcroft, in addition to valley mills at Burrs and Deeply Vale.

In 1838 the Parish of Walmersley was established, and a church was built just beyond the junction with the turnpike. It was an austere building in the style of a chapel and furnished with a gallery, but it served a growing population well. A school was built close by in the following year.

In 1873 Walmersley was declared one of the most prosperous and flourishing parishes in the Diocese, and in the same year it received a new incumbent, the Reverend John Davies Evans. By now the local population had grown to 4,000, and a new church building (36804, opposite) came under consideration. It was designed in neo-Gothic style by the local architects Maxwell and Tuke, and was completed in 1883. A tower and spire were added in 1913 in memory of Canon Evans.

WALMERSLEY CHURCH, THE INTERIOR 1895 36805

The nave of Walmersley church. The window above the chancel was taken from the earlier church.

RURAL BURY- ELTON

OF the five townships that made up the parish of Bury, Elton was second only in population to the Bury township itself, and until 1825 its boundary stretched almost to the centre of Bury at Castlecroft. Here Peel had established his mills on the eastern bank of the River Irwell in 1773, and here at Chamber Hall his son, the future Prime Minister, was born, in Elton - not in Bury, as history would have it.

But the majority of the population lived in scattered communities to the west of the river. Brandlesholme Hall held much of its history, having been in the possession of the Greenhalgh family for over four hundred years. John had been a close aide to Charles I during the Civil War, but he survived Cromwell's Commonwealth, and the Greenhalghs remained at Brandlesholme until 1728.

Elton's early industries grew along the banks of its streams: the Elton Brook, the Walshaw Brook and the Woodhill Brook. An estate map of 1775 shows crofts along the Elton Brook where cloth would be bleached, an industry that benefited from the pure waters flowing off the moors. Here at Elton Vale the Rothwells established their business, later to be succeeded by the Whiteheads.

In 1796 the canal had arrived from Bolton and Manchester, and by the early years of the 19th century industry was growing. In addition to ever larger cotton mills, Joseph Webb established an iron foundry in 1846. Charles Walmersley built his Atlas engineering works in 1866, and papermaking was in production at Cromptons in 1856 and at Olives, in Woolfold, around 1880.

From 1846 Elton had become a part of the Parliamentary Borough of Bury. It was soon to become one of the borough's busiest workshops.

Above: ELTON, ALL SAINTS' CHURCH, THE INTERIOR 1896 37388

Opposite: ELTON, ALL SAINTS' CHURCH 1895 36787

The growing population of Elton prompted the building of All Saints' Church on a bluff of land known as Goose Hill Bank. The church with its distinctive tower was designed by John Harper, who also designed two other Bury churches, Saint Marie's and Saint Paul's. £2,500 was raised by public subscription, and land was granted by the Earl of Derby. It took almost two years to build, and was consecrated by the Bishop of Chester on 29 June 1843. The church was illuminated by a supply from the nearby gas works, of which the vicar was a shareholder. Two years later Lord Derby granted more land for the building of a school (seen in the distance to the right) 'for the education of Children or Adults, or Children only of labouring, manufacturing and other poorer classes in the township of Elton'. The school was opened on 4 September 1847 and provided a basic education for infants and children, many of whom were part-timers in the local mills. In the early years of the 20th century the 'scholars' were absorbed into the newly-opened council schools, but Sunday School classes remained at All Saints' and the building became the Parish Hall, a centre for many memorable events. In recent years the congregation has met at St Francis House in Brandlesholme and the old church has been converted to private apartments, but many of the gravestones in the churchyard carry the names of those who once brought prosperity to the township.

RURAL BURY - WALSHAW AND TOTTINGTON

TOTTINGTON TODAY is a growing residential community, but a century ago it was a typical industrial township on the outskirts of Bury. Yet it had an impressive historical pedigree. It had been an extensive manor held by the de Montbegons after the Norman Conquest, but after passing to the de Lacys in 1235 it was divided into two parts: Tottington Higher End and Tottington Lower End. Alice de Lacy married Thomas, Earl of Lancaster, but had no male heir, and the manor became part of the Honour of Lancaster. Under Henry IV it became crown property and carried the impressive title 'Royal Manor of Tottington'. Bury, in contrast, had been a minor manor held in the 12th century by Adam de Bury 'for one Knight's fee'.

WALSHAW HALL 1895 36806

Thomas Baron was a fustian manufacturer in Walshaw in the 17th century. The first Walshaw Hall was built by his son Peter around 1740. It was demolished in 1844, and replaced and enlarged in the ornate style of the Victorian era. In 1876 James Kenyon, a leading textile manufacturer with mills in Bury and Heywood, took his new wife to live at Walshaw Hall and established a long tradition of Kenyon occupancy stretching across many generations. It became a centre of social life not only for the family, but for many of their employees. When the Kenyons left it became a residential home for the elderly.

RURAL BURY - WALSHAW AND TOTTINGTON

Within the boundaries of Tottington Lower End would have been the much humbler settlement of Walshaw, a scattering of cottages and farmsteads among winding country roads. But by the 1840s the establishment of two cotton mills, Holts and Haworths, were to transform its fortunes. When James Haworth came to the village, he opened a shop where the Victoria Inn stands today and 'put out' work for handloom weavers. The Haworths later built a mill nearby, operated by James' son Jesse, for the manufacture of fustians. Despite difficult times during the cotton famine in 1860, he was able to provide work and 'schooling' for his employees and was well respected in the village.

Walshaw never grew beyond its needs, but in 1891 the Co-op built a row of shops at the corner of Bank Street. The Co-op has now gone, but above the sturdy facade we can still see carved in the stonework 'Grocer', 'News Room' and 'Clogger'. There is little need for a clogger in Lancashire today.

WALSHAW, CHRIST CHURCH 1895 36807

When Jesse Haworth died in 1887 at the age of 83, his nephew, the Rev John Gorell Haworth, together with his aunt, Nancy Haworth, proposed that an Anglican church be built at Walshaw in his memory. The Rev Haworth had established a Sunday School in the village in 1847, but was now the vicar of a parish in Rossendale. The Jesse Haworth Memorial Church was subsequently built, and was consecrated in 1889.

RURAL BURY- HOLCOMBE

HOLCOMBE once lay in the Royal Hunting Forest of Rossendale, and its history is steeped in the hunting tradition. In Norman times there were severe laws protecting the King's forests, and any breach of them was met with severe penalties. For the aristocracy and the gentry, however, hunting was a popular sport. The de Trafford family built Hey House at Holcombe in 1616 as a hunting lodge.

When James I came to Lancashire a year later, he was so impressed by the Holcombe Harriers that he decreed that henceforth they should wear tunics of pink and gold. It is a privilege which has been upheld to the present day.

James I would, perhaps, have been less impressed with the reputation that Holcombe was to acquire in later years. In 1789 William Sheldrake, a poet, complained

HOLCOMBE HILL 1896 37390

The Hare and Hounds at Holcombe Brook clearly has close associations with the Holcombe Hunt; but it is a busy place for many visitors during the summer months, not least on Good Friday, when crowds gather before making the traditional climb up the hill beyond.

77

of 'moral mischief' at the annual festival known as the Wakes. At this time there would have been dog fights, cock fights and bull baiting, and Sheldrake speaks of 'excessive drinking and self-indulgent behaviour'. Following the Wakes of 1800, the vicar complains of the locals spending most of the day in the fields and the inns before coming to church. There was certainly no shortage of inns: the White Hart, the Black Bull, the Blue Bell, and the Shoulder of Mutton were in the village on the hill and the Hare and Hounds was down in Holcombe Brook.

During Victorian times the celebrations became more restrained, but the tradition is still upheld today: on Good Friday crowds assemble to climb the hill, and perhaps climb the tower erected in 1852 to honour Sir Robert Peel following his repeal of the Corn Laws.

Holcombe Church 1896 37389

Emmanuel Church, Holcombe, has a long ecclesiastical history. The de Montbegons had granted lands to the Priory of Monk Bretton in Yorkshire in the early 13th century to build a chantrey at Holcombe to provide shelter and a place to pray for pilgrims travelling to Whalley Abbey. Chantries were suppressed under Edward VI, and for a time Holcombe depended on Bury for its ministry. It was restored during the reign of Queen Elizabeth I in a building which was once a court house and prison. It was enlarged in 1774, but was finally demolished in 1851. The present building was consecrated by the first Bishop of Manchester on 8 April 1853.

RURAL BURY- RAMSBOTTOM AND THE GRANTS

IT IS SAID that when the Grants came down from Scotland in 1783, they gazed across the valley at Ramsbottom and it reminded them of their native Speyside.

But the Grants were heading for Manchester in search of work. Meanwhile, it was Robert Peel (the father) who was setting up mills in Ramsbottom (at that time the district was still a part of Holcombe). But by the turn of the century, the Peels were moving away; the Grants, who had now prospered, bought their mill on the 'Old Ground'. In the same year, 1806, they bought the house at Top o'th' Brow and renamed it Grant Lodge. Soon they were expanding, and in 1812 they purchased Allsops cotton mill and the old hall at Nuttall. Five years later, John Grant was to build a new hall on the site of Shipperbottom Farm (37391, below). In 1821, they

NUTTALL HALL AND GRANT'S TOWER 1896 37391

We can see Nuttall Hall on the left, with its tower hinting at the Scottish Baronial style. To the right was the coach house and stables. On the hill above stands Grant's Tower at a point known as Top o'th' Hoof.

built Square Mill only a short distance from their estate, situated by the river and designed to withstand the industrial unrest that threatened at the time.

But the Grants continued to prosper, and in 1827 William and Daniel had a tower built high above the valley (37391, page 79) in memory of their parents. It survived until 1944, when it collapsed owing to neglect. They were themselves immortalised by Charles Dickens as the Cheeryble Brothers in 'Nicholas Nickleby'. The Grants have long gone, and so, too, has their Hall and the mill at Nuttall, but their old residence still flourishes as the Grant Arms in the centre of the town.

NUTTALL BRIDGE 1896 37392

Nuttall Bridge, spanning the River Irwell as it flows towards the Gollinrod valley, was built by the Grants to link the Hall with their mill.

The Cemetery 1895 36798

The Church of England chapel.

RURAL BURY - REST AND RECREATION

BY THE MIDDLE of the 19th century the graveyard at Bury parish church was full to capacity, and its position in the centre of the town clearly presented a health hazard. There were rumours of a new burial ground, but the Improvement Commissioners were reluctant to face the taxpayers with the expense. In 1852, however, following two major cholera epidemics, the Government passed the Burial Act. An inspector visited Bury two years later, and immediately closed the graveyard, declaring it a threat to public health.

But it was to be another fifteen years before Bury had a cemetery; it was built on land obtained in the township of Redvales. It was, however, designed on a grand scale by the Borough Surveyor James Farrar and the Manchester architect Henry Styan, with a chapel for each of the denominations: Anglican (36798), Roman Catholic (36799, page 84) and Non-conformist (36800, page 84). It was formally opened on 21 May 1869, and the first interment was on 18 September - that of Joseph Downham, aged 81, a cabinet maker of Trinity Street. Of its 33 acres, over a third was set aside for pleasant walks amid flower beds and shrubbery, as it was the Victorian concept that such places should provide as much for the refreshment of the soul as for the passing of the body.

The Cemetery 1895 36799

The Roman Catholic chapel.

The Cemetery 1895 36800

The Non-conformist chapel.

WALMERSLEY ROAD RECREATION GROUND 1895 36795

This is Clarence Park in Walmersley Road. A stylish Victorian Tudor gatehouse was provided for the park keeper, and no park was complete without its elegant bandstand.

ROCHDALE ROAD PARK C1955 B257023

Here we have a tranquil scene in Rochdale Road Park, but Mr Openshaw's gymnasium is nowhere to be found.

RURAL BURY - REST AND RECREATION

Proposals for recreation grounds where 'plots of land be enclosed for playgrounds for children' were first considered by Bury councillors in the early 1880s, but were again delayed by financial uncertainties. It was left to a private benefactor, the ubiquitous Henry Whitehead, to offer land in Elton to create a park in memory of his mother. Thus Bury's first public recreation ground was opened in May 1886, with the condition that henceforward the Corporation would be responsible for its maintenance.

By now enthusiasm was growing, and the authorities proposed the building of three more recreation grounds within the Borough, the first to be in Rochdale Road (B257023, page 85). A public subscription was opened, and Thomas Openshaw gave 5 acres of land together with provision 'for pleasure gardens and a gymnasium'. The grounds were opened in July 1888 by Prince Albert Victor, eldest son of the Prince and Princess of Wales, amid much celebration.

With the support of an offer of £10,000 from Lord Derby, Clarence Recreation Ground in Walmersley Road (36795, page 85) was opened shortly afterwards, to be followed by another in Manchester Road. Within three years some 20 acres of land had been acquired by charitable donations to create public parks in the borough.

GRANT'S TOWER FROM BROOKSBOTTOM 1896 37393

Finally, here is a pastoral scene: the waters of the Irwell flow down from the deep wooded valleys that contour much of the landscape of south-east Lancashire. But industry is never far away. Between the trees we can glimpse the smoking chimney of Joshua Hoyle's cotton mill, and to the left are the rows of terraced houses that he built for his workers. On the distant hilltop Grant's Tower stands to remind us of the mill-owners and their workpeople, who by their enterprise and labour moulded much of the history of Bury and its townships.

Names of Subscribers

The following people have kindly supported this book by purchasing limited edition copies prior to publication.

In memory of my dear Mum & Dad, love Anne
Mr & Mrs Battle, Bury, Lancs
To my sons and daughter. Frank Brierley
Gillian Brooks
To Roy Burton, Bury, on his birthday
To Mark Caldwell, love Mum
Doreen Cockayne
To Dad, from Joanne, Steve and Jack
The Fletcher Family, Bury
To Chris, Daniel, Gillian and Robert Powell
Ethel Hart
Councillor David M Higgin, Bury MBC
Victoria Jackson and Family, Bury
Memories of Fred Jessup, Bury
Valerie Johnson
The Kay Family, Bury and Heywood
Mr & Mrs R W Kitchen & family, Bury
The Lamb family, Bury
The Mapplebeck Family - Bury
To Margaret, from Ethel, Edith and Colin
To Dad, Trevor Mason, on your birthday
Susan and Colin McCardell
J P McCleary, Bury
Stephen McDonald

James McDonald
Harry and Betty Mills
Carol & Barrie Morton
Lorraine, Alastair and Liam Nuttall
Mr and Mrs A Parker
Philip James and Jeanette Proctor
Asha & Gautam Rawat
Pat Read, née Greenhalgh, Unsworth
George William Reed
In memory of Alt & Ethel Salmon of Bury
The Salmon Family, Hollins, Bury
Robert Settle
Janet Marjorie Shannon & family
Mr & Mrs Sidebottom, Bury, Lancs
Edith and Colin Taylor, Bury
Barrie and Bernadette Taylor
George Vail, Bury
Stephen, Karen, William and James Vale 2006
Frederick C Wilkie, Whitefield, Manchester
Birthday Congratulations.
  D R Wilson Farnham, 43
The Wolfenden Family, Bury
Mr & Mrs R N Yates, Cockey Moor

FRANCIS FRITH'S
TOWN&CITY
MEMORIES

FRITH PRODUCTS & SERVICES

Francis Frith would doubtless be pleased to know that the pioneering publishing venture he started in 1860 still continues today. Over a hundred and forty years later, The Francis Frith Collection continues in the same innovative tradition and is now one of the foremost publishers of vintage photographs in the world. Some of the current activities include:

Interior Decoration

Today Frith's photographs can be seen framed and as giant wall murals in thousands of pubs, restaurants, hotels, banks, retail stores and other public buildings throughout the country. In every case they enhance the unique local atmosphere of the places they depict and provide reminders of gentler days in an increasingly busy and frenetic world.

Product Promotions

Frith products are used by many major companies to promote the sales of their own products or to reinforce their own history and heritage. Frith promotions have been used by Hovis bread, Courage beers, Scots Porage Oats, Colman's mustard, Cadbury's foods, Mellow Birds coffee, Dunhill pipe tobacco, Guinness, and Bulmer's Cider.

Genealogy and Family History

As the interest in family history and roots grows world-wide, more and more people are turning to Frith's photographs of Great Britain for images of the towns, villages and streets where their ancestors lived; and, of course, photographs of the churches and chapels where their ancestors were christened, married and buried are an essential part of every genealogy tree and family album.

Frith Products

All Frith photographs are available Framed or just as Mounted Prints and Posters (size 23 x 16 inches). These may be ordered from the address below. From time to time other products - Address Books, Calendars, Table Mats, etc - are available.

The Internet

Already ninety thousand Frith photographs can be viewed and purchased on the internet through the Frith websites and a myriad of partner sites.

For more detailed information on Frith companies and products, look at this site:

www.francisfrith.com

See the complete list of Frith Books at:
www.francisfrith.com
This web site is regularly updated with the latest list of publications from The Francis Frith Collection. If you wish to buy books relating to another part of the country that your local bookshop does not stock, you may purchase on-line.

For further information, trade, or author enquiries please contact us at the address below:
The Francis Frith Collection, Frith's Barn, Teffont, Salisbury, Wiltshire, England SP3 5QP.
Tel: +44 (0)1722 716 376 Fax: +44 (0)1722 716 881 Email: sales@francisfrith.co.uk

---

See Frith books on the internet at www.francisfrith.com

FREE PRINT OF YOUR CHOICE

Mounted Print
Overall size 14 x 11 inches (355 x 280mm)

Choose any Frith photograph in this book.
Simply complete the Voucher opposite and return it with your remittance for £2.25 (to cover postage and handling) and we will print the photograph of your choice in SEPIA (size 11 x 8 inches) and supply it in a cream mount with a burgundy rule line (overall size 14 x 11 inches).
Please note: photographs with a reference number starting with a "Z" are not Frith photographs and cannot be supplied under this offer.
Offer valid for delivery to one UK address only.

PLUS: Order additional Mounted Prints at HALF PRICE - £7.49 each (normally £14.99)
If you would like to order more Frith prints from this book, possibly as gifts for friends and family, you can buy them at half price (with no additional postage and handling costs).

PLUS: Have your Mounted Prints framed
For an extra £14.95 per print you can have your mounted print(s) framed in an elegant polished wood and gilt moulding, overall size 16 x 13 inches (no additional postage and handling required).

IMPORTANT!

These special prices are only available if you use this form to order. You must use the ORIGINAL VOUCHER on this page (no copies permitted). We can only despatch to one UK address. This offer cannot be combined with any other offer.

Send completed Voucher form to:
The Francis Frith Collection, Frith's Barn, Teffont, Salisbury, Wiltshire SP3 5QP

CHOOSE A PHOTOGRAPH FROM THIS BOOK

Voucher for **FREE** and Reduced Price Frith Prints

Please do not photocopy this voucher. Only the original is valid, so please fill it in, cut it out and return it to us with your order.

Picture ref no	Page no	Qty	Mounted @ £7.49	Framed + £14.95	Total Cost £
		1	Free of charge*	£	£
			£7.49	£	£
			£7.49	£	£
			£7.49	£	£
			£7.49	£	£
			£7.49	£	£

Please allow 28 days for delivery. Offer available to one UK address only

* Post & handling	£2.25
Total Order Cost	£

Title of this book . . . .

I enclose a cheque/postal order for £ . . . .
made payable to 'The Francis Frith Collection'

OR please debit my Mastercard / Visa / Maestro card, details below

Card Number

Issue No (Maestro only)   Valid from (Maestro)

Expires   Signature

Name Mr/Mrs/Ms . . . .
Address . . . .
. . . .
. . . .
. . . . Postcode . . . .
Daytime Tel No . . . .
Email . . . .

ISBN 1-84589-155-4   Valid to 31/12/08

Free Print – see overleaf

Can you help us with information about any of the Frith photographs in this book?

We are gradually compiling an historical record for each of the photographs in the Frith archive. It is always fascinating to find out the names of the people shown in the pictures, as well as insights into the shops, buildings and other features depicted.

If you recognize anyone in the photographs in this book, or if you have information not already included in the author's caption, do let us know. We would love to hear from you, and will try to publish it in future books or articles.

Our production team

Frith books are produced by a small dedicated team at offices in the converted Grade II listed 18th-century barn at Teffont near Salisbury, illustrated above. Most have worked with The Francis Frith Collection for many years. All have in common one quality: they have a passion for The Francis Frith Collection. The team is constantly expanding, but currently includes:

Andrew Alsop, Paul Baron, Jason Buck, John Buck, Jenny Coles, Heather Crisp, David Davies, Natalie Davis, Louis du Mont, Isobel Hall, Chris Hardwick, Julian Hight, Peter Horne, James Kinnear, Karen Kinnear, Tina Leary, Stuart Login, Sue Molloy, Sarah Roberts, Kate Rotondetto, Eliza Sackett, Terence Sackett, Sandra Sampson, Adrian Sanders, Sandra Sanger, Julia Skinner, Lewis Taylor, Will Tunnicliffe, David Turner and Ricky Williams.